MW01008706

ℋomeward

B·O·U·N·D

Al-Anon Family Group Headquarters, Inc.
New York, NY 1993

Contents

This Is For You!

Now, at last, someone close to you is in treatment or some other facility and is about to return home. This booklet is designed to help ease the transition — for everyone concerned.

The one you love is getting help, but what about you? After all, you have adjusted and readjusted so many times. You may be tired. You may have questions about alcoholism, treatment, and the changes recovery brings.

The fact is that it's not only the alcoholic who gets sick from the disease — the whole family is affected. They deserve to get well; you deserve to get well also.

Al-Anon and Alateen members are relatives and friends of alcoholics who have discovered that sharing experience, strength, and hope with one another builds both courage and confidence. Our purpose is to help anyone whose life has been affected by someone else's drinking. Attendance at meetings, reading Al-Anon literature, and sharing with other members helps to bring serenity and happiness into our lives.

You may never have attended an Al-Anon or Alateen meeting before, or you may be slightly familiar with the program. In either case, this booklet is for you. It's a place to turn for guidance and reassurance — a place to share with people who have experienced what you are going through now.

We believe you will find in these pages answers to some of your questions and, more importantly, real reasons to believe Al-Anon will offer you courage, strength, confidence and hope.

Our Way Of Welcoming You: Members Share

A D U L T   C H I L D

I did not believe the Al-Anon program could help. I was unique — or so I thought. Both of my parents are active alcoholics, and when my mother entered a rehabilitation center, I had to face the facts.

Not only had I been unable to prevent my parents from drinking, but I had spent so much time focusing on them that I finally "hit bottom." I will always be grateful to a friend who pointed me to Al-Anon.

At my first meeting, I learned I was powerless over my parents — and that all I could do was live my life, one day at a time. The people in the room were so warm and friendly that it made me apprehensive. They told me to keep coming back, so I did.

Gradually, I learned to "Live and let live." Because of this, my relationship with my parents — even my relationship with my sisters — has improved. I have become more honest. I now understand that I was not the only family member affected by alcoholism.

When I came into the program, I thought living my own life meant abandoning the alcoholics in my family. I was afraid — and lonely. Today I have a successful career and many wonderful friends. By learning how to lovingly "let go" of my parents, I have been given a wonderful gift: a life of my own.

PROGRAM IN ACTION

Focusing on myself.
Learning I cannot change or control anybody but myself.
Understanding what it means to "let go."
Learning to live "One day at a time."

I am the mother of two alcoholic children. When they went through treatment, I found Al-Anon and realized how much I had been affected by alcoholism. I had reached the point where I simply did not know what was right. I had allowed my children to manipulate me.

The merry-go-round began to stop when my husband and I found the Twelve Steps. At meetings, we started to talk about our feelings and realized we weren't the only ones with problems. The lines of communication were opened.

Our family is celebrating its fourth anniversary in Al-Anon and AA this year. We each have our own sponsors to help us with our programs. Being in Al-Anon has been a great growing experience, though sometimes painful. Change is not always easy or instant.

By working the program, my family is now pulling together instead of pulling apart.

PROGRAM IN ACTION

Finding and using my sponsor.
Being willing to change.
Working the program
(reading, going to meetings, using the phone).

I was numb, frozen in my feelings, trying to remain "invisible" at Al-Anon meetings. This was my pattern in life, learned from my family. "Don't feel, don't talk, don't get close, don't become a part of anything" were the unspoken rules for survival.

What pain and grief and shame I felt! I was not living or growing. My denial, and the various barriers I had erected, kept me stuck; I was just existing. These walls were gradually broken down by just attending meetings.

Over time, I could verbalize the word "alcoholism" — I could admit that my son was an alcoholic and that I had grown up in an alcoholic family. Gradually, my trust grew to the point where I could reach out to others. Now I call people daily on the telephone; I maintain a relationship with a supportive sponsor, and I am following the Twelve Steps toward a lifetime of recovery.

PROGRAM IN ACTION
Calling other Al-Anon members.
Using my sponsor.
Letting the Twelve Steps guide my way.

Members Share On:

What is it like when someone first returns from treatment?

SPOUSE

My wife was in a 30-day treatment program, and when she returned home, I was not prepared. I expected she would be sober, and she was. However, she was a different person from the one who had gone off to treatment. In fact, she was a different person from the one I had known in our many years of marriage.

She was a stranger. We could not communicate very well, and we both felt ill at ease. Later, she confided she was afraid I would not accept her and her newfound sobriety.

I know that I was fearful, too. My personality had changed over years of reacting to alcoholism. I did not know I had choices on whether or not to react. As a result, I developed high blood pressure. I was physically and emotionally sick.

So there we were — two people separated by alcoholism, two people who had become strangers, two people needing to get better — each in our own ways.

Fortunately, I found meetings where people shared their experience, strength and hope with me. I began to feel better. My wife and I became closer. We had to fall in love again to start building a new and better marriage. With the help of the Twelve Steps, we did.

PROGRAM IN ACTION

Attending meetings regularly.
Remembering I have choices.
Letting the understanding, love, and peace of the program
grow in me.

When my husband returned from treatment, I didn't want to make waves for awhile because I didn't want to rock his boat. Then I began attending Al-Anon meetings where I learned to keep my eyes on myself. When I did this, I found I had less time to worry about him.

The Slogans became my life raft and the Serenity Prayer my life vest. Of course, there are still choppy seas. But with the help of my program, my sponsor, and all my friends in Al-Anon, the sailing is smoother now, and things are better than they have ever been before in my life.

PROGRAM IN ACTION

Focusing on myself.
Using the Serenity Prayer.
Remembering to "Live and let live."
Finding a sponsor and using my sponsor.

My son is an alcoholic. When he went into treatment, I felt both hopeful and afraid. I thought, "If it works, great — but what if it doesn't?" Such thoughts were constantly on my mind the first few weeks.

After participating in Al-Anon meetings at his treatment center, my world became less frightening for me. I began to realize that his time in treatment was my time to get help — we both needed to get better.

When he returned home, I focused on how we were both improving through our respective programs. I told my son I loved him, but not his disease. Today I know better than to trust the disease, but I have learned to trust my Higher Power. Daily I put myself into my Higher Power's hands, and I do the same with my son. And if there is one thing I can say, it is this: we are in good hands.

PROGRAM IN ACTION

The First Step (I can't).
The Second Step (God can).
The Third Step (I think I'll let Him).

Members Share On:
Why do I need help — there's nothing wrong with me!

PARENT

When my 19-year-old son entered a correctional facility, I returned to Al-Anon. I was able to receive support from others who had walked in the same shoes and who could really understand.

I had been swallowed up by someone else's problems. With help, I was able to look at myself rather than try to control the behavior of another person. I was able to concentrate on my own life.

Al-Anon taught me to detach with love instead of anger and to look at what I could do, such as write letters to my son and visit him. My program helps me remember that I love my son, but I must allow him to be responsible for his own problems.

PROGRAM IN ACTION

Being responsible for my problems and not those of someone else.
Changing the things I can.
Remembering "Easy does it."

I always seemed to date boys who were alcoholics. Whenever I was dating someone who wasn't, I felt like I wasn't worthy of him.

Then I found myself dating someone in treatment. He always blamed me for his drinking, and soon I began to believe that I really was the cause of it. He never believed he had a problem, so treatment didn't help him. The relationship soon ended.

In Alateen I learned it was not my fault. The meetings helped me understand that alcoholism is a disease, and there was nothing I could have done to stop his drinking. I keep coming back because I see how far I have come.

PROGRAM IN ACTION

Learning The Three C's:
"I didn't cause it, I can't control it, and I can't cure it."
Accepting the fact that alcoholism is a disease.
Learning to change the things I can — namely me.

*A*fter many years of steady drinking and worsening behavior, my wife entered a rehabilitation unit. An orientation program was held for families on Thursday nights. Naturally I attended — I felt it would help the alcoholic.

The Chairperson was a delightful woman who told us about Al-Anon and how it had helped her. She touched on the Twelve Steps and the Twelve Traditions and shared how her life had become so much better when she attended Al-Anon.

I, however, felt it was my wife who had the problem. I could not understand why I needed to attend Al-Anon. I continued only because I felt it would help her.

Truly, I got little if anything from those meetings. The Chairperson did manage to get a commitment from me — I promised her I would go to a men's Al-Anon meeting. To my amazement, I found 25 to 30 men of all ages when I got there. Apparently it was then I realized I was not the only man in my state with an alcoholic wife. What a weight was lifted off my shoulders!

Sixteen years later, I still regularly attend meetings. Why? Because I find people there who apply Al-Anon principles in all their affairs. It is not an exaggeration to say that my entire life has been changed by learning to do this in my life as well.

PROGRAM IN ACTION

Attending meetings regularly.
Studying the Twelve Steps and the Slogans.
Practicing these principles in all my affairs.

When my son was in jail, I would lie awake at night and pray that God would just let me die. The pain I felt was too great. I felt like a failure as a mother.

Two years in the program have changed my thoughts. Listening to others has taught me that I was being "overly responsible." Just as I cannot perform surgery, I cannot fix alcoholism — or anyone with it. I have learned to place my son in his Higher Power's care and re-mind myself daily that my Higher Power is the great physician.

I continue to attend Al-Anon meetings because I need them. I go to exercise classes to keep my body fit; I go to Al-Anon to improve my spirituality.

PROGRAM IN ACTION

Changing what I can — namely me.
Trusting my Higher Power.
Attending Al-Anon meetings.
The Second Step.

Members Share On:
How can I help ease things at home?

ADULT CHILD

I had mixed feelings when my mother went into treatment after many years of drinking. In some ways, I felt angry and resentful about her drinking; in other ways, I felt relieved that she was finally getting help. The meetings I attended at the treatment center helped me get in touch with my whole mixed bag of feelings — I even discovered feelings I did not realize I had.

In meetings, I was able to express my worries about what to say and do when my mother returned home from treatment. I developed an understanding of the damage alcoholism had caused my whole family. And I gradually grew to appreciate the fact that I have no control over my mother or her alcoholism.

Al-Anon has helped me learn to allow my mother to tend to her own business, while I tend to mine. Thankfully, we are both experiencing wonderful success — one day at a time.

PROGRAM IN ACTION

The First Step.
Remembering to keep my focus on me.
Learning to live "One day at a time."

When my husband came out of the hospital, I still continued to keep track of what he was or was not doing. I would look for the age-old signs of when he was going to start drinking again. I kept track of the meetings he attended, and when I didn't feel he was going often enough, I would panic.

In Al-Anon I learned, little by little, to "let go" of him and let God look after him. Then I started to focus on myself and my own recovery. I began to see that my anger, bitterness, and shattered expectations were more destructive to me than to anyone else.

Originally, it was pain that brought me through the doors of Al-Anon. Now, several years later, the sense of belonging and the gift of serenity are the reasons I keep coming back.

PROGRAM IN ACTION

Taking the focus off the alcoholic and looking at myself.
Remembering to "Let Go and let God."

I have been going to Alateen meetings for nearly two years. I started going because of my father's drinking problem. Now I go to help myself.

Before I came to Alateen, I was always blaming myself and others for my father's drinking. I learned that my father has the disease of alcoholism. I felt angry, lonely, ashamed, and embarrassed. Alateen helped me talk about my feelings, especially when my dad got home from treatment. It helped me to stop worrying about what to say and how to act because I had learned that I can't make him stop drinking. Only he can do that.

PROGRAM IN ACTION

Hands off!
Alcoholism is a disease.
Acceptance.
Talking about my feelings.

*F*ive years ago, my two sons (ages 14 and 16) were placed in a treatment center. That was when I discovered I am an adult child of an alcoholic; my life had been affected by the alcoholism of both my father and my sons.

It was suggested that I go to Al-Anon meetings on a regular basis. I couldn't get there fast enough because I knew I would get better — and I am, step by step.

As I kept coming back, I began to hear people talk about everyone having a "Higher Power." If everyone has their own Higher Power, I thought, then I could entrust myself to mine — and everyone I love to theirs. I decided to give it a try.

"Detach with love" began to make sense. At first, it was difficult to keep the focus on myself. But I have been practicing a long time now, and it is getting much easier and so is my family environment. We have a new closeness among us, because we are using the principles of the program in our daily lives.

PROGRAM IN ACTION

The Second Step.
The Third Step.
Detaching with love.
Remembering to "Live and let live."
Remembering to work my program.
The Twelfth Step.

Members Share On:
Should I try to protect the alcoholic?

PARENT

Nine months have elapsed since my daughter's last treatment, and I have had lots of opportunities to practice Al-Anon. For example, as she began to run around with a drinking crowd, I paused to use the slogan "Think." I also reflected on the principle of detachment. These tools helped me avoid becoming a victim of runaway emotions.

Learning to operate this way was difficult for me, especially because the principles I was applying were often contradicted by messages from my spouse and society. I have finally learned to listen for guidance from my Higher Power instead.

Today, my relationship with my daughter is based on love and honest communication. We have agreed that she is responsible for her own life and recovery — and I am responsible for mine.

PROGRAM IN ACTION

Remembering to "Think, decide, then act."
Practicing the principle of detachment.
Listening for guidance from my Higher Power.
Remembering to keep the focus on myself.

*A*s my husband's return from a treatment center approached, I was concerned about the bottles that were still in our house. I wasn't sure if I should give them away before he came home (so as not to tempt him) or leave them there (and hope he would not succumb).

Confused and fearing that whatever decision I made would be wrong in my husband's eyes, I finally asked an Al-Anon member for guidance. His loving reply was this: "Ask your husband what he would like. That way, he'll be making the decision."

What a "Keep it simple" answer! I applied the suggestion, which put the responsibility of my husband's sobriety on him, right where it belonged. He decided to keep the bottles there, because, he felt, he had to get accustomed to a drinking world. Of course, I worried to some extent, but knew that learning to trust had to start somewhere. I felt peace knowing the choice was his and not mine.

PROGRAM IN ACTION

Remembering to "Keep it simple."
Remembering that everyone has their own Higher Power.
Learning to entrust people to their Higher Power —
and myself to mine.
The Third Step.

I spent many years trying to protect my son. I changed him from school to school; I selected his teachers; I screened his friends, telephone calls, activities. When I finally did let him assume responsibility, it was not until after he had been through three treatment centers.

The way I coped was to spend more and more time at work and I isolated from friends so that I wouldn't have to share my son's problems. I grew to feel negative about myself, the alcoholic, and life in general. I felt hopeless and trapped in the situation. I would not confide even in my family members. I kept my son's treatment programs secret and would not share his disease with anyone. I felt guilty, ashamed, and worthless for having an alcoholic son.

I did not learn of Al-Anon until the third treatment center. Part of the program consisted of Al-Anon meetings for family members. It was there I encountered the Twelve Steps, the Serenity Prayer, the Slogans — and learned to share problems with members of the group. I actually became a serious, practicing member of Al-Anon.

Unfortunately, even this third round of treatment failed — my son relapsed. But this time, I knew where to go for support and how to cope with the disease. I would not go down with him this time.

The tools of the program that keep me alive today are a combination of working the Twelve Steps, the Slogans, and going to meetings. While there, I listen and share. I continue to learn (from newcomers and long-time members) that recovery is a process, not a single event. As I share my powerlessness, I also help myself get out of my head and place the problem on the table. By working the Steps, I'm able to continually process my problems and move to yet another level of acceptance. Prayer and meditation assist me daily.

PROGRAM IN ACTION

The Steps and Slogans and the Serenity Prayer.
Sharing and listening at meetings.
The process of recovery.

Members Share On:
What if the alcoholic drinks again?

PARENT

After having lived with the drinking problems of my son through high school, junior college, marriage, divorce and the loss of jobs, I was the one who wound up in the coronary unit of a major medical facility. That was when I was referred to Al-Anon.

At first, I wasn't sure Al-Anon was where I belonged. I went because I needed to do something about my son's drinking. But Al-Anon members kept telling me I was there for myself. Over and over, I heard "The Three C's": I did not cause alcoholism, I cannot control it, nor can I cure it.

After several months, the members' sharings started to make sense. I began to set boundaries. I realized I loved my son, but not his disease. I started to see changes as I worked through the Twelve Steps — changes in me. My son has not found sobriety, but I have found a new life of serenity — a life without the anger, fear, and resentments I had when I first reached out for help.

PROGRAM IN ACTION

Not accepting unacceptable behavior.
Realizing I have choices — and that it is up to me to take care of myself.
Remembering "The Three C's."
Asking for courage to change the things I can — namely me.
The Fourth Step.

I thought life would be great when my dad came out of the 28-day treatment program. Then he stopped going to AA meetings. I had nightmares about him drinking again. Well, the nightmares came true.

I learned I was powerless over alcohol and that I had my own life to lead. So I kept reading my literature, talking to people, going to Alateen, and thinking about myself — not the alcoholic.

That is the best thing I could have done — for him, for me, for both of us.

PROGRAM IN ACTION

First Step.
Detaching with love.
Reading Alateen literature.
Focusing on myself.

*M*y husband was in a treatment center for a month, and during that time, I spent three weekends in family treatment. It was a wonderful way to begin, a safe place to explore feelings and also start to communicate with the alcoholic.

He went to AA meetings every night and I went to Al-Anon just as much. After three months, he drank again and then several more times after that.

It took me nearly a year-and-a-half of good, solid Al-Anon to really accept that it was his problem and not mine and to overcome my feelings of impending doom.

Maybe I thought our lives would be lived "happily ever after" once he returned home from treatment. But, finally, I came to realize that I can only take care of myself. If he drinks, it's his disease and he has to come to terms with it. What I can do is live my life and do what I need to do in order to live it well.

PROGRAM IN ACTION

Acceptance.
Setting limits.
Taking care of myself.
Remembering to "Live and let live."

I was first introduced to Al-Anon several years ago by a recovering alcoholic who worked in a mental health facility. I thank the God of my understanding for this. I had gone to the facility begging for help because I had been through two bad alcoholic marriages and was now faced with another severe drinking problem — this time, it was my 14-year-old son. My boy had been locked up twice for driving under the influence. As a plea bargain, he agreed to go through a rehabilitation program.

When he was first released, he went to meetings and appeared to be trying. After that, he just quit going to AA and now he is drinking again.

I thank God for the Al-Anon program. It has made me strong enough to mean what I say and say what I mean. I am still his mother — I can't divorce him — and am naturally concerned about his well-being. But I am able, on most days (one day at a time) to practice "Letting go and letting God." I now know with my head and heart that I cannot change or control him. Above all, I have learned that I can recover, whether he is still drinking or not.

Saying what I mean — and meaning what I say.
Remembering to "Let go and let God."
Living my life "One day at a time."
Learning I am powerless over everyone and everything —
except myself.

Members Share On:

How can I rebuild my relationship with the alcoholic?

SPOUSE

I was the mother of four young children when my husband was institutionalized. I read about Al-Anon in a newspaper column and became a member immediately. But that doesn't mean I relinquished control right away. It took me about ten years to be able to do that.

It came gradually. It wasn't until five years ago that I truly learned to surrender and trust my Higher Power. Probably because of that, my husband has finally come to grips with his disease.

Al-Anon is helping me "just for today" — giving me the tools I need to focus on taking my inventory, not that of anyone else. Through both of our programs, we have a very good relationship today — one day at a time.

PROGRAM IN ACTION

Learning that I am powerless.
The Fourth Step.
The Tenth Step.
Just for today.
One day at a time.
The Serenity Prayer.

My husband had been sent to a treatment center by court order after many years of drinking. The treatment center had a family program and I was urged to attend.

Two people from the Al-Anon program came in and talked about their new life. I had been to Al-Anon two years before, but I wasn't ready to accept the program.

This time it was different! I was able to take what I liked and leave the rest — whatever I didn't understand. Soon I found myself attending as many Al-Anon meetings as I could.

When my husband was released from treatment, we were both nervous. We didn't know what to expect. We were different people and had to learn to communicate again. I wondered if things would work, if we could rebuild our marriage. It was hard for me to "let go" and not try to control everything.

I said the Serenity Prayer over and over many times. We were both attending our own recovery programs. It was consoling to know that others had done this before me — and that I could make it too.

PROGRAM IN ACTION

Attending meetings to "Listen and learn."
Learning to "Let go and let God."
Saying the Serenity Prayer.

My mother had a drinking problem that affected the whole family. Some years after I started Al-Anon, she went into treatment.

Al-Anon helped me better understand my part in the disease and to continually try to turn my mom over to the Higher Power — before, during and after her treatment program. I didn't try to control her as I might have in the past — I needed to resist my tendency to judge, accuse, and manage. I kept turning her over to her Higher Power — and asking my Higher Power to help me keep my focus on me.

I was thrilled, amazed, and thankful when my mother decided to seek sobriety. But Al-Anon told me to focus on myself. So, while I am very grateful for my mother's continuing recovery, I am thrilled, amazed, and thankful for mine.

PROGRAM IN ACTION

The First Step.
The Second Step.
The Third Step.
Having an "attitude of gratitude."

Members Share On:
How can I stop being angry and afraid?

YOUNGER FAMILY MEMBER

I remember my dad drinking ever since my mother died. I thought he never understood me. I couldn't take it anymore — that's why I started going to Alateen. Through this program, I have found myself and I have started to feel good about me.

I like the idea of talking to a group because I'm a "people person." I feel comfortable with the group; I feel better knowing that I'm not alone. A lot of teens have the same problems I do.

I look forward to Alateen all week long. It makes my life better. It helps me cope with everyday life and its problems.

PROGRAM IN ACTION

Taking care of myself.
Learning to "Live and let live."

I was angry and afraid when my spouse entered treatment. I felt as if my whole world was tumbling down around me. I was enraged because I thought my spouse now had an excuse for all of his absurd behavior. I also felt scared and guilty because I thought I had made him an alcoholic.

The treatment center staff suggested I go to Al-Anon. I wanted Al-Anon to tell me they could cure my husband. What they told me instead was this: my husband has a disease. They gave me literature to read and talked to me.

I could not believe what I read — my life in print! So much of what had happened in my home was in the Al-Anon literature, and I could relate to what the members shared. For the first time, I did not feel alone.

I read all the Al-Anon literature I could get. I kept going to meetings and talking to members. As I began to reach out for the help I desperately needed, my anger and confusion began to subside. Sobriety scared me: I didn't know how to act, what to say, how to feel or what to do. But with the help of Al-Anon, I was able to face it all and I am so grateful I did. Anger and fear no longer rule my life.

PROGRAM IN ACTION

Applying Al-Anon literature.
Talking to members.
Listening and sharing at meetings.
Reaching out for help.

When my wife entered treatment, the counselor asked if I had any resentments. I remember saying "no!"

Today I am grateful that counselor pointed me to Al-Anon — for the patience of the Al-Anon group who tolerated me and that they didn't ask me to leave! I talked a lot and told others how they should live their lives.

Eventually the Twelve Steps, the Twelve Traditions, the Serenity Prayer, the Slogans and opportunities for Al-Anon service work made me a new person. The resentments that had been so apparent to everyone but me are considerably lessened, and I am now living my own life. I try to follow the Twelve Steps and, though difficulties still occur in my life, I am different now in how I deal with them.

PROGRAM IN ACTION

The Twelve Steps and Traditions.
The Serenity Prayer and Slogans.
Working the program.
Getting involved in service work.

I did everything for my ex-husband except breathe for him. In return for all that controlling and enabling, what did I get? Pain, humiliation, and shame. My life was a blur of misery — full of anger and fear.

Al-Anon came into my life at the time he entered a treatment center. I went because it was "an assignment." The family counselor stated that we could not participate in the after-care program if we did not go to Al-Anon. So I went — grudgingly.

There they told me if I did not keep coming I would most likely marry another alcoholic. Believe me, that was enough to keep me coming back!

My recovery began with Step One, which told me I was powerless over alcohol, people, places, and things. That helped me see I was not responsible for the alcoholic — or his disease. I began to "let go" of him and concentrate on what needed to be changed in myself.

Today, five years later, I am still recovering. Where I had anger, fear, resentments and almost hatred, now I have a large measure of peace, freedom, and happiness.

PROGRAM IN ACTION

Detaching from the alcoholic.
Taking care of myself.
Learning that I am powerless over others.
Continuing to work my own program of recovery.

Members Share On:
What shall I say to the children?

SPOUSE

I came into Al-Anon because of my husband. His disease had progressed to the point where his employer demanded he get help. I remember how I felt when he went into the hospital. I was scared and so were our six children. I didn't know what to say to them.

Fortunately, I had been in Al-Anon for four years. So when the children asked me every day if he would stay sober, I could tell them I had no answer — that his sobriety was his responsibility.

We began to attend Al-Anon meetings as a family, which brought us closer to one another. My husband came home on Thanksgiving Day. I remember how we all sat around the dining room table as he read a letter of amends he had written to us all. We cried, hugged, and sat down to dinner together. There were still many fears and doubts in all of us, but we were glad he was home.

The children and I continue on our respective roads to recovery, while the alcoholic works on his. Recovery is a road we travel, not a destination. It helps all of us to remember that.

PROGRAM IN ACTION
Reading the Twelve Steps daily.
Remembering that "We never graduate."

*I*t was easy to deceive myself into thinking that the children didn't really know what was going on. But when I got honest enough to take a hard look, I could see they did indeed know — they knew something was terribly wrong.

I decided to explain the disease by comparing it to my son's allergy to peanuts. I pointed out that alcoholism makes people sick, like allergies to peanuts. I told them it wasn't their mother's fault that she is sick — and that she can't help what she is saying when she is drinking.

I was amazed at their ability to deal with the truth. Shrouding the disease in mystery had been frightening for them — much more frightening than our down-to-earth talk.

· PROGRAM IN ACTION

Alcoholism is a disease.
Honesty.

Members Share On:
What will I get out of the program?

PARENT

My son was finally institutionalized for his drinking problem. Until then, I had spent my life begging his teachers and principals to give him a second, third, fourth, fifth chance. I did his homework for him so he wouldn't fail. I talked to school counselors, friends, youth ministers, and local police about how to change his behavior.

I had not given my son any responsibilities. But I had yelled, cried, begged, demanded, laid guilt trips, tried to understand, grounded, blamed — all in my efforts to straighten him out.

In utter defeat, despair and hopelessness, my husband and I took him to a psychiatric hospital for treatment. There I was told to go to Al-Anon — that it would help my son when he came home. So I went — not for me — but for my son.

After awhile, I started to enjoy the meetings. I was making friends. Life wasn't just what I should be doing — it was what I wanted to do. I was in the embryo stage of developing a life of my own.

When my son returned home, it was Al-Anon that helped me avoid the chaos and turmoil of how it had been before. Now I knew how to avoid being obsessed with his problems and crises. I learned to say what I mean and mean what I say. When he told me he hated me, I said, "That's OK — I'd rather have respect than love." His old tricks don't work anymore because I have new tools that do.

PROGRAM IN ACTION
Learning to keep my focus on myself.
Setting limits.
Not trying to control anyone but myself.
Learning to detach with love.

*T*hirteen years ago, my husband was hospitalized for alcoholism. An Al-Anon meeting was held at the hospital, and I attended. I am grateful today because the Al-Anon members helped me to keep myself together during this difficult time. They gave me the hugs, love, and most of all the hope that I needed. Their stories helped me feel less alone.

The tools I learned in that first Al-Anon group are the ones I still use now: the Serenity Prayer which is reinforced by "Let go and let God," the wonderful daily readings, the Slogans and the Steps. These tools keep me from doing things that might be detrimental to myself.

PROGRAM IN ACTION

The Serenity Prayer.
Learning to "Let go and let God."
Reading daily from Al-Anon literature.
Working Al-Anon's Twelve Steps.

*T*he first thing I learned in Al-Anon was that I could not change an-other person and that I was powerless over alcohol. This was really good to hear because I had been trying so hard to somehow stop my mother's drinking.

I then learned that I could only change myself. Unfortunately, I strived to become a perfect person and failed. So, I stopped attending Al-Anon meetings.

Seven years ago, when I was 25, I hit bottom. I hadn't attended an Al-Anon meeting for at least a year-and-a-half. Nothing else had helped, however, so I reluctantly returned to the Al-Anon rooms.

This time, I tried to practice the Steps and Slogans, even though I did not feel capable of doing so. I finally mustered the courage to mention how I felt — and found that almost everyone in the room had felt the same way. No one criticized me; they told me how I felt was OK. Their acceptance and unconditional love helped me more than anything else at that time. The concern I saw in their eyes and the smiles I received are something I don't believe I ever will forget.

PROGRAM IN ACTION

The First Step.
Doing all I can — and leaving the rest to God.
Minding my own business.
Attending meetings regularly.

I always knew there was something wrong with my father. It was when a friend introduced me to Alateen that I became aware of his alcoholism and began attending Alateen meetings regularly.

I remember the awakening I experienced when I went to my first meeting. I was welcomed with open arms. The support and warmth I received helped me learn to express myself — and change myself — successfully.

My father has never gone into the program or attempted to recover. Living with an active alcoholic has certainly not been easy, and it has only been Alateen and good friends that have gotten me through. Since my dad is still drinking, it is important that I practice detachment. That is what allows me to love him, despite his disease.

Meetings give me the chance to identify with others. The Slogans help me to stop for a moment and "Think." The shared hope, strength, and unconditional love are the things that keep me coming back.

PROGRAM IN ACTION

Changing the things I can.
Detaching with love.
The Slogans.
Attending Alateen meetings regularly.

Members Share On:

Is there any hope of finding happiness again?

SPOUSE

*T*wo years ago, my alcoholic husband was sent to prison for four months. We had just bought a house and were in the process of re-modeling it.

I had never felt so helpless and deserted in my life. I was scared, angry, hurt, and embarrassed all at the same time. The contractors would ask me to make decisions about the house. I had no clue what to do, so I would close my eyes, get in touch with my Higher Power and then tell them my decision.

My Al-Anon meetings were a great support. I was constantly re-minded that this too was one of life's learning experiences for me and that God doesn't give us anything we can't handle.

After much hard work, the house was finished and my husband came home. Now, two years later, we are both working our respec-tive recovery programs. Today I believe that with the help of my Higher Power and the Al-Anon program, I can handle anything.

PROGRAM IN ACTION

The Second Step.
The Third Step.
Remembering I am not alone.

did not accept Al-Anon until some time after my son entered treatment. It took me awhile to admit I was powerless and that I too needed help.

After several meetings, I was beginning to feel comfortable as the only male in a group of twenty or so women. At first I didn't talk as freely as they did. Gradually, I realized that my feelings and attitudes were much the same as theirs.

My "comfort level" was further raised when I recognized service work as a part of my recovery. The Twelve Steps and the Slogans became very helpful, especially in my learning to live "One day at a time." I was constantly reminded to "Let go and let God." I found, too, that things were never as important as I made them, and I could truly "Live and let live."

Finally, my son accepted AA and went back to college. He worked hard and stayed sober for six years before a heart attack took his life. When he died, some thoughts went through my mind as to whether or not to continue attending Al-Anon. After I went back to my home group, I had no more doubts. The love and compassion shown to me there are things I cannot receive anywhere else.

Today, all I need to do is follow the Twelve Steps and accept the good that is in the program for me.

PROGRAM IN ACTION

The Twelve Steps.
Slogans.
Attending Al-Anon meetings regularly.

I'm not one who remembers dates, but I remember the date of my first Al-Anon meeting when I walked in feeling alone and hurting and I walked out feeling I had found something important for myself.

I didn't like what was said because I was finding very little positiveness in the world. I didn't like being told that if I hurt it was my choice and my attitude. Yet on some level I knew it to be true.

As dejected as I was, I was able to see that there were people in Al-Anon who seemed relaxed with themselves — people who could sit and smile. I wanted that. I wanted to feel alive and OK.

I now understand what the Al-Anon fellowship offers. The Twelve Steps are leading me, and I, too, am feeling alive and OK.

PROGRAM IN ACTION

Remembering that I have choices.
Going to meetings to "Listen and learn."
Trying to apply the principles of the program daily.

P A R E N T

*M*y 17-year-old daughter went to a treatment center because of her alcoholism. This is when I was introduced to Al-Anon. What I saw and heard there made sense to me.

The Al-Anon program has given me a new and better way to live. The Slogans were my first tools. I used "Easy does it" the most — I had to slow down. Then "Let go and let God" became a lifesaver for me. I had to put my daughter in the hands of the Higher Power because I couldn't do anything to help her; I had to help myself.

Today I'm living "One day at a time" to the best of my ability. The program has given me a lot — but mostly, it has given me ME.

PROGRAM IN ACTION

Easy does it.
Let go and let God.
One day at a time.
Taking care of me.

The Transition From Family Treatment Into Al-Anon

The transition into recovery from the effects of alcoholism is never easy — for anyone concerned. New meetings mean new places, new faces, and a slightly different approach from the meetings you attended in the treatment center. It helps to be patient — to bear in mind that family treatment gave you discovery; Al-Anon will give you recovery.

In Al-Anon meetings, we speak from the heart — in simple, everyday terms. You will probably hear a different kind of language in your home-based meetings — people sharing about feelings and experiences and how they are using the tools of the program in their lives. You will also notice that members make contributions at meetings — but they are voluntary, and there is no cost for membership in Al-Anon.

There are some less visible aspects of the program. Al-Anon does not support or recommend any particular treatment centers, therapeutic techniques, counselors, therapists — or publications other than Al-Anon Conference-Approved Literature (which we affectionately call "CAL"). Two precious gifts of the program are anonymity and confidentiality, both necessary to create a comfortable climate in our meeting rooms, where we can share with one another. At Al-Anon meetings, we usually put it this way, "Whom you see here, what you hear here, when you leave here, let it stay here."

In making the transition to home-based meetings, remember that recovery in Al-Anon is a process, not a destination. It takes a while to learn that we can be as happy as we allow ourselves to be, to realize that we can live our own lives to the fullest — regardless of whether the alcoholic is drinking or not.

It has been our experience that it takes time for newcomers to get past the basics, so — be patient with yourself. Keep attending meetings, letting the understanding, love, and peace of the program surround you. Let Al-Anon grow in you, one day at a time.

A Few Special Words

*A*l-Anon has many terms you may already be familiar with — but here are some (with a few brief definitions) to help you get started:

Anonymity. Each person should be able to leave an Al-Anon meeting secure in the knowledge that who they saw and what they heard will remain confidential.

Disease. For the alcoholic, alcoholism is a physical, emotional, and spiritual disease. It is a family disease because all who are close to the alcoholic are affected.

Detachment. Detachment results from learning to separate ourselves from the effects of another person's alcoholism and behavior.

Higher Power. The God of our understanding.

Service. It is possible to support Al-Anon in a variety of ways that help others find the program. Members often say "To keep what we have, we have to give it away."

Sponsor. A person with whom to discuss personal problems or questions — someone who will, in return, share their experience, strength, and hope in guiding us with the program.

Twelve Steps. Twelve principles of recovery, adapted from Alcoholics Anonymous, are the foundation of the Al-Anon program. They help us to improve our lives and our relationships with others.

Working the Program. Applying Steps, Traditions, Slogans and the Serenity Prayer to our lives — reading Al-Anon literature, attending meetings, talking with a Sponsor, calling members between meetings.

Some of the Slogans of Al-Anon

JUST FOR TODAY
Regretting the past and fearing the future is pointless. In Al-Anon, we try to live just one day at a time — and to live that day as fully as we can.

FIRST THINGS FIRST
This is a reminder to set priorities, giving precedence to those things that are most important to us.

EASY DOES IT
Tension and impulsive action only lead to trouble. Slowing down keeps us more relaxed and, thus, makes us more productive and useful.

LIVE AND LET LIVE
This reminds us to live each day fully by focusing on ourselves — always respecting the fact that other people have their own opinions and are responsible for their own actions.

LET GO AND LET GOD
When we have done everything we feel we can do, we then turn to our Higher Power to ask for help in finding solutions.

LISTEN AND LEARN
To change our attitudes, we need to hear them. God works through people, so, by listening to others, we gain awareness and insight. By listening to ourselves as well, we hear how we need to change. Listening — and learning from the listening — is what leads us to action, growth, and change.

KEEP IT SIMPLE
This reminds us to focus on what is immediately in front of us without making the situation or task more complicated than it really is.

KEEP AN OPEN MIND
To develop new attitudes and a new way of life, our thinking must expand. We learn to catch ourselves being narrow-minded or trying to control, and we become open to exploring new ways of thinking by applying Al-Anon ideas.

A Few Suggestions

ON REACHING OUT

Find out how to contact Al-Anon locally. Get Al-Anon phone numbers and lists of meetings when you attend so you can contact someone when you need to talk. Feel free to ask questions — even of Al-Anon members who are total strangers. You can also contact people after meetings.

ON RECOVERY

You can change — your life can change. It may not change the way you expect, but no situation is hopeless and things will get better. Members often recommend attending at least six meetings before making a decision as to whether you like Al-Anon. Try visiting different groups, as meetings vary in flavor and size.

Attend as many meetings as you can to accelerate your understanding of the program and how it can help you. Try not to be impatient.

ON FEAR AND PROJECTION

Projecting is about "what ifs" that may never come to pass. The past has passed, and the future hasn't happened yet, so try to focus on right now and how best to use it.

ON SPONSORSHIP

Listen and look for someone you would like to help guide you through the Twelve Steps and your growth in the program. You might find it helpful to get a temporary sponsor to talk with in the early days until a more permanent sponsor is found.

ON DAILY READING

It is helpful to use Al-Anon Conference-Approved Literature (CAL). Read, for example, from one of our daily readers, *One Day At A Time* or *Courage To Change*, or in more detail about our program, *Al-Anon's Twelve Steps and Twelve Traditions*.

ON ATTENDING AL-ANON REGULARLY

Keep coming back. You are in the right place. Everyone in the fellowship started as a newcomer, and everyone remembers how it is in the beginning. We are here for you — to listen and to share our experience, strength, and hope. Our own progress is proof that the program works — if only we work it.

The Twelve Steps

The Al-Anon program is based on the Suggested Twelve Steps of Alcoholics Anonymous, which we apply to our own lives:

1. We admitted we were powerless over alcohol—that our lives had become unmanageable.

2. Came to believe that a Power greater than ourselves could restore us to sanity.

3. Made a decision to turn our will and our lives over to the care of God *as we understood Him.*

4. Made a searching and fearless moral inventory of ourselves.

5. Admitted to God, to ourselves and to another human being the exact nature of our wrongs.

6. Were entirely ready to have God remove all these defects of character.

7. Humbly ask Him to remove our shortcomings.

8. Made a list of all persons we had harmed, and became willing to make amends to them all.

9. Made direct amends to such people wherever possible, except when to do so would injure them or others.

10. Continued to take personal inventory and when we were wrong promptly admitted it.

11. Sought through prayer and meditation to improve our conscious contact with God *as we understood Him,* praying only for knowledge of His will for us and the power to carry that out.

12. Having spiritual awakening as the result of these Steps, we tried to carry this message to others, and to practice these principles in all our affairs.

The Twelve Traditions

*T*hese guidelines are the means of promoting harmony and growth in Al-Anon groups and in the worldwide fellowship of Al-Anon as a whole. Our group experience suggests that our unity depends upon our adherence to these Traditions:

1. Our common welfare should come first; personal progress for the greatest number depends upon unity.

2. For our group purpose there is but one authority—a loving God as He may express Himself in our group conscience. Our leaders are but trusted servants; they do not govern.

3. The relatives of alcoholics, when gathered together for mutual aid, may call themselves an Al-Anon Family Group, provided that, as a group, they have no other affiliation. The only requirement for membership is that there be a problem of alcoholism in a relative or friend.

4. Each group should be autonomous, except in matters affecting another group or Al-Anon or AA as a whole.

5. Each Al-Anon Family Group has but one purpose: to help families of alcoholics. We do this by practicing the Twelve Steps of AA *ourselves*, by encouraging and understanding our alcoholic relatives, and by welcoming and giving comfort to families of alcoholics.

6. Our Al-Anon Family Groups ought never endorse, finance, or lend our name to any outside enterprise, lest problems of money, property and prestige divert us from our primary spiritual aim. Although a separate entity, we should always cooperate with Alcoholics Anonymous.

7. Every group ought to be fully self-supporting, declining outside contributions.

8. Al-Anon Twelfth-Step work should remain forever nonprofessional, but our service centers may employ special workers.

9. Our groups, as such, ought never be organized; but we may create service boards or committees directly responsible to those they serve.

10. The Al-Anon Family Groups have no opinion on outside issues; hence our name ought never be drawn into a public controversy.

11. Our public relations policy is based on attraction rather than promotion; we need always maintain personal anonymity at the level of press, radio, TV and films. We need guard with special care the anonymity of all AA members.

12. Anonymity is the spiritual foundation of all our Traditions, ever reminding us to place principles above personalities.

Index